GERMAN FIGHTERS OVER RUSSIA

Snow is thrown-up by the propeller of this FW 190A-4 as it moves out on another sortie. Both aircraft are FW 190A-4s of I/JG 54 (625/3194/2).

BRYAN PHILPOTT
GERMAN FIGHTERS OVER RUSSIA

WORLD WAR 2 PHOTO ALBUM NUMBER 16

A selection of German wartime photographs
from the Bundesarchiv, Koblenz

PSL Patrick Stephens, Cambridge

First published in 1980

British Library Cataloguing in Publication Data

German fighters over Russia – (World War 2 photo
  albums; no. 16).
  1. World War, 1939–1945—Aerial Operations, German-
  Pictorial works
  2. World War, 1939–1945—Campaigns-Russia-
  Pictorial works
  3. Fighter planes—Pictorial works
  I. Philpott, Bryan II. Series
  940.54′21   D787

ISBN 0 85059 424 3 (casebound)
ISBN 0 85059 423 5 (softbound)

Photoset in 10 pt Plantin Roman. Printed in Great
Britain on 100 gsm Pedigree coated cartridge
and bound by The Garden City Press Limited,
Letchworth, Hertfordshire SG6 1JS, for the
publishers, Patrick Stephens Limited, Bar Hill,
Cambridge, CB3 8EL

CONTENTS

Acknowledgements
The author and publisher would like to express their sincere thanks to Mrs Marianne Loenartz of the Bundesarchiv for her assistance, without which this book would have been impossible.

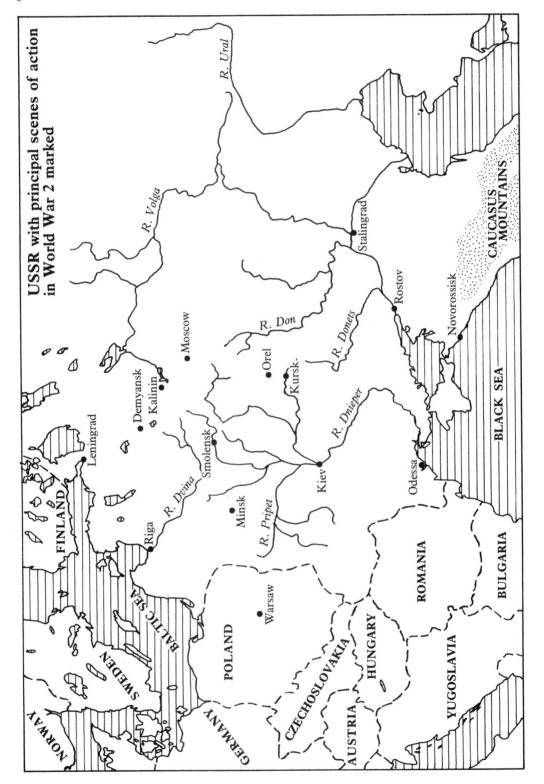

USSR with principal scenes of action in World War 2 marked

In early 1943 two FW 190s of I/JG 51 were returning to their base after having successfully engaged Russian Pe 2 twin-engined bombers which had been attacking German armour and infantry. Low on fuel and ammunition, both pilots kept a watchful eye for Russian fighters, which were now becoming more of a handful than they had been in the early days of the Eastern campaign. Suddenly, the leader spotted what he thought was a stray FW 190 several thousand feet below; believing that strength in numbers would help the singleton, he pulled his aircraft into a diving turn that placed his Rotte at the same level as the other aircraft. Levelling out, the German pilots discovered that the stray was a Russian LaGG 3 whose pilot appeared to be oblivious of their presence. The leader concentrated on placing the Russian squarely in his gunsight while the wingman kept a watchful eye for other Russian fighters. Just as the FW 190 pilot fired his remaining ammunition the LaGG whipped into a turn and the deadly fusilade went harmlessly by its wingtip. Both aircraft became engaged in an aerial ballet, neither giving or asking any quarter, then with fuel states critical, the engagement ended. As the Russian turned away the German pilot saw that long fair curls protruded from beneath the pilot's helmet and he realised that his adversary was a woman.

The two JG 51 flyers returned safely to base and duly reported what they had seen; probably being the first two German fighter pilots to encounter female opposition at the controls of a high performance fighter aircraft. So was entered another unusual happening in a campaign that through the years has brought its own legends—some true, some fiction—about fighter pilots; especially those flying for the Luftwaffe.

Many writers have attempted to dismiss the impressive scores of the Luftwaffe 'Experten' accumulated in Russia as being figments of the imagination, hollow victories achieved against obsolete aircraft flown by peasants, or duplicated claims; these are inaccurate generalisations and are nowhere near the truth.

In 1941 when the German offensive against Russia was launched, the Luftwaffe had a total of 920 fighters supporting 1,085 level and dive bombers and most of the fighter pilots were men of experience who had seen action in the West and the Middle East. Ranged against them was the world's largest air force, over 8,000 combat aircraft in 23 air divisions. But numerical strength is misleading and it must be remembered that the Great Purge had robbed the Soviet Air Force of many of its leaders, replacing them with inexperienced officers or, worse still, men appointed for political reasons. The rapid expansion of the Russian air divisions brought a hurried training programme resulting in many aircrew being far from fully trained or having the necessary expertise when they took their places in front line squadrons. Nonetheless, the 4,000 aircraft which were ranged along the expected front of the German attack, although comprised mainly of obsolescent biplane and monoplane fighters, did have a sprinkling of aircraft of modern design such as the Yak-1, MiG 3 and LaGG 3 among them. What the crews lacked in experience they tried to make up for in the honour of defending their homeland; sadly in the initial thrusts this was not enough and many Russian pilots died needlessly as their leaders threw them into hopeless battles.

Although warned by various sources that a German attack was imminent, the Russians took no steps to disperse their forces, and consequently the Luftwaffe's initial strike at dawn on June 22 1941 resulted in row upon row of Russian aircraft, ranged as though for inspection on 31 forward fields, being destroyed. This first strike underlined the Luftwaffe's main role as a tactical weapon designed to support the ground forces by laying a carpet of devastation through which they could advance with relative impunity. So far the proven tactic of fighters to clear the opposition, level bombers to soften the ground forces, then dive bombers to wreak havoc, had worked in every campaign except the one against England.

Luftwaffe crews returning from the opening round of Operation 'Barbarossa' hardly had time to relive their triumphs before their aircraft were refueled, rearmed and returned to the fray. This time they did meet some aerial opposition in the form of Soviet fighters which, numerically, seemed to be as plentiful as ever, despite the huge numbers destroyed on the ground during the initial strikes. The I-153, I-15 and I-16 fighters were all inferior in performance to the Bf 109s which totally equipped the Luftwaffe's single-engined fighter units, but at low level they were much more manoeuvrable and soon began to present problems to the German pilots. Leutnant Schiess of JG 53 found himself well placed to open his account in Russia, but just as he was about to open fire, the I-16 in his gunsight was pulled into a full 180 degree turn and was heading straight for the Bf 109 with all guns blazing. The quality of the Russian fighter pilots may have been lacking in some respects, but as far as courage was concerned they seemed to be endowed with more than their fair share, as was demonstrated to an unfortunate crew of a ZG 26 Bf 110 which was rammed by Senior Lieutenant Kokorev of the 124th Fighter Regiment when the guns of his I-16 jammed.

At the end of the first day the Luftwaffe was well on top with staggering claims of 322 aerial victories and a total of 1,489 Soviet aircraft destroyed on the ground. On the debit side 35 Luftwaffe aircraft were missing, among which was that of the Kommodore of JG 27, Major Wolfgang Schellman, who in shooting down an I-16 could not avoid flying through the wreckage of his victim which so damaged his Bf 109 that he had to abandon it. At this time Schellman had 25 victories and, although his parachute descent was uneventful, it was subsequently discovered that he had been shot by his captors—a fate that sadly was to befall many Luftwaffe aircrew who fell into Russian hands. On a happier note, Oberstleutnant Werner Mölders, the popular Kommodore of JG 51, was given an immediate award of the Swords to his Knight's Cross with Oakleaves, for shooting down four Russian aircraft; a multiple claim that was not unusual on the opening day of the Russian campaign.

At this point it is worthwhile considering the claims made by Luftwaffe pilots and the general reasons why their victories, particularly in Russia, were so substantial.

For at least the first two years of the campaign the Germans enjoyed total air superiority as far as equipment was concerned. At the start of Operation 'Barbarossa' all Jagdgruppen equipped with single-engined fighters had Bf 109s, the majority of these being the greatly improved F version, although the units still using the older E variant were by no means at a disadvantage. Aerodynamically the F was a 'cleaner' aircraft than the E, but the early models were fitted with only two 7.9 mm MG 17 machine-guns and a rather odd calibre (15 mm) MG 151 cannon. Although the fire rate of the cannon was relatively high, it did not produce the firepower needed, and consequently pilots used to the heavier armament of the E quite often felt dissatisfied with their newer aircraft and at one stage there was a danger of tlpis affecting morale. The arrival of the F-4 version in August 1941 redressed the balance since this aircraft used a 20 mm MG 151 which, although firing at a slower rate, had far greater 'punch'. Later of course the FW 190 and Bf 109G arrived on the scene and these were generally superior to anything the Russians had, including fighters supplied on Lend/Lease. The fighter leaders responsible for the Jadgruppen on the Eastern Front were all vastly experienced pilots and tacticians; many of them traced their combat experience to the Spanish Civil War, as well as the campaigns in France and particularly the Battle of Britain where they had found a tenacious foe who met them on equal terms. Many of the pilots serving under these officers also had considerable experience and had been in combat since the opening days of the war. The German system was very much based on the individual skills and successes of the fighter pilot, and the Luftwaffe hierarchy placed considerable importance on total victories achieved; often basing the award of decorations and promotion on such attainments. Fighter pilots were taught sound tactics from their early days at the training schools, and the Luftwaffe perfected the 'finger four' formation which was eventually adopted and adapted by the RAF and USAAF. Another extremely important factor was that once a pilot joined his squadron he stayed with it for his service life; breaks came with official leave, or the whole unit being temporarily withdrawn to rest or re-equip, but there was no set number of hours or operations before temporary respite from combat came in a training school or behind a desk. It is easy to understand, therefore, that any pilot who happened to be a skilful flyer, an average marksman, and whose unit was in the right place at the right time, stood a very good chance of obtaining a score higher than those associated with western aces.

In Russia the German fighter airfields were very much forward bases and therefore much nearer the field of operations; thus time over the target was increased as was combat duration, but conversely turn around time was decreased, so it was not unusual for a pilot to carry out up to eight sorties a day and be engaged in combat on every one. One of the classic examples often quoted to prove this point is that of Leutnant Scheel of JG 54, who joined his unit in May 1943 and flew 70 sorties during which he shot down 71 aircraft, before being killed on July 16 1943.

The proximity of the fighter bases to the front also enabled quick confirmation to be obtained both from ground and aerial sources, thus double claims and overclaiming were brought to reality.

The Soviets, apart from the elite guards units, were nowhere near as well trained as the Luftwaffe pilots and certainly did not have the tactical awareness needed in a good fighter pilot. Another very important factor was that the Soviet Air Force was used almost exclusively in a tactical role, so the onus of interception, bringing with it height, speed and sun position advantage, therefore more-or-less always became the exclusive right of the Jagdgruppen.

It is advisable to keep this overall picture in mind when reading or discussing Luftwaffe fighter pilots' claims; it applies basically to a certain degree to all fronts, but is totally applicable to the Russian campaign.

During the first week of 'Barbarossa' 4,017 Russian aircraft were destroyed for a cost of 179 Luftwaffe machines and many fighter pilots were beginning to get the impression they were at a 'Turkey shoot', and the race was on to see who would be the first to achieve what was then the magic total of 100 victories. On the 30th of the month, as the German army's armoured columns closed a pincer movement around the Russian stronghold of Minsk, the Soviet Air Force mounted a massive air raid in an attempt to prevent the impending disaster.

The Jadgruppen of Kesselring's Luftflotte 2 had a field day, especially the pilots of JG 51, and the unescorted Russian SB-2s and DB-3s were decimated. At the end of the day JG 51 had become the first unit to achieve 1,000 victories since the opening days of the war in September 1939, and of the

114 Russian bombers accounted for, the redoubtable Mölders claimed five bringing his personal tally to 82. Hauptmann Joppien and Leutnant Heinz Bär, two names which were to become household words in Germany, also recorded five kills each in the action and kept themselves well in the hunt to be the first to 100. Joppien never reached the target as two months later, with his score at 70, of which 28 had been achieved in Russia, he was killed in action. Somewhat predictably the first man to reach his century was Mölders and he did this on July 15 with his 33rd Russian victory which took his overall total to 101, plus 14 in the Spanish Civil War.

The rivalry between individual pilots became reflected in their units as each victory accredited to the Jagdgruppen brought pride to all personnel.

In support of the Army Group North, Major Trautloft's JG 54, which was part of Keller's Luftflotte 1, saw little of the early action but by the end of June was well into the fray as the Russians attempted to cut off the 4th Panzer Group's line of advance by bombing the Düna bridges. The Grünherz Geschwader, as it was known, continued to support the advance of the Army Group right to the gates of Leningrad, becoming the third unit to reach 1,000 victories on August 1 having just been beaten to second place by JG 53. Later the same month Major Günther Lutzlow's JG 3, operating with Luftflotte 4, also reached the 1,000 kill mark, thus spreading the successes equally over the Luftflotten.

The incredible losses suffered by the Russians, who in addition to the Luftwaffe were now facing units of the Finnish, Rumanian, Hungarian, Slovakian and Italian air forces, did not appear to have any affect on morale or supply and it became very evident that defeat would never be conceded and the German army supported by the Luftwaffe would have to fight every inch of the way to a victory which they believed was theirs for the asking. In fact, replacement aircraft were reaching the Russians at a phenomenal rate, flowing from the factories during the latter part of 1941 at four times the rate they had in the first six months of the year. Among them were LaGG 3 and Yak-1 fighters, both of which were now coming in sufficient numbers to eventually cause the Luftwaffe serious problems, and alongside them the formidable Il-2 ground attack aircraft which was so hard to shoot down and which was to take a devastating toll of German armour, was also reaching a high production rate. The fact that the Russian factories were able to boost their output to three times the pre-war rate in just under 12 months and record a total aircraft production of 15,735, under-lines just how the lack of a strategic bombing plan, or indeed an aircraft to undertake such a plan, was to cost Germany the war. Such production rates were not confined to the aircraft industry, and it is worth pondering the point that later in the campaign one week's operations against Russian armour would account for only one day's output of T-34 tanks, against which also had to be offset the Luftwaffe ground attack, bomber and fighter losses. Training of new crews went on undisturbed, so gradually a formid-able force was being built up in the sanctuary of peace-like conditions well away from unwelcome and disruptive attention.

This, of course, was not appreciated by the Luftwaffe front-line units, who daily found more and more Russian bombers and fight-ers engaged on what appeared to be a hope-less quest.

In September 1941 RAF Hurricanes arrived at Murmansk, 39 of them in two squadrons, Nos 81 and 134, forming No 151 Wing, arriving on the first Arctic convoy. Realising that convoys taking supplies to Russia would be within easy striking dis-tance for the Luftwaffe, the allies obtained permission to operate Hurricanes in defence of the port of Murmansk with the proviso that the aircraft would eventually be handed over to the Red air force. No 151 Wing there-fore formed the vanguard of a massive Lend/Lease programme from the western nations.

The Hurricanes were in action for the first time on September 11 when they lost one of their number to Bf 109Es of JG 77. The Hurricane was the most modern fighter so far encountered by the Jagdgruppen on the Russian front, but even in the hands of a well-trained RAF pilot it was still at some disadvantage against the nimble Bf 109s; nonetheless, when the Russians took over the aircraft their pilots gave a good account of themselves and were certainly able to fight on more even terms. The Hurricane's fam-ous partner of the Battle of Britain, the Spit-fire, also found its way to Russia in consider-able quantity, the first of a total of 1,188 arriving in December 1941 and taking part in the defence of Moscow.

Throughout the summer and early autumn the German advance continued and the Luftwaffe played an important part not only in attaining air superiority, but also con-taining pockets of Russian resistance which had been by-passed by the advancing armour to be dealt with by the back-up infantry. Such exertions cost the Luftwaffe dearly for both fighter and ground attack pilots soon found to their cost that Russian infantrymen did not immediately seek shelter when con-fronted by a strafing aircraft but fired back at it with any small arms available. Such ac-tivity, coupled with the extremely accurate anti-aircraft fire, greatly contributed to the total loss of 1,600 German aircraft in the first three months of the campaign, and severe damage to another 1,028, the grand total being practically equivalent to the strength of the Luftwaffe committed at the opening of 'Barbarossa'. The failure of the German air-craft industry to achieve a production rate that would compensate for such losses, underlined the failure of Udet who in November 1941 could no longer face the mounting problems and committed suicide. He was replaced by Milch who immediately overhauled the whole system, but increased production was a long way off and in fact too late to really help.

The Russian winter found the Luftwaffe ill-prepared and aerial activity declined as aircraft became unserviceable and spares, due both to lack of production and com-munication, failed to reach the front line units. During December the assault on Mos-cow was finally abandoned as the full force of the Russian winter hit the Germans hard, but it did not have the same affect on the Rus-sians and much to the surprise of the Luft-waffe, the Soviet air force became very active as the Russians went on the offensive.

A decline in Axis fortunes in the Middle East resulted in Luftflotte 2 being deployed to that theatre in December 1941 and among the fighter units involved were three Grup-pen of JG 53, part of JG 3 and III/JG 27; coupled to this several other Jagdgruppen were sent back to Germany for re-equipping, the overall result being a considerable reduc-tion in fighter units available. This, together with the deplorable weather, is reflected in the drop in claims and awards made to fighter pilots during the close of 1941 and early 1942. By the time the renewed summer offensive began in June 1942 fortune had again favoured the Axis in the Mediterranean enabling them to redeploy units to Russia and strengthen them with newly equipped elements from Germany. Fighters now in use were all late mark Bf 109Fs although the FW 190A was beginning to be seen in increasing quantities after a disappointing debut in the winter of 1941.

The emphasis in the fighter pilot's war was again turned to individual success and the race was on to see who would be first to reach 200 victories, the 150 barrier having been passed for the first time in August 1942 by Major Gordon Gollob of JG 77. In no other campaign was there so much importance and publicity placed on the achievements of individuals and by mid-1942 a definite pattern was emerging within the Jagdgruppen. Within each unit a handful of pilots would emerge as being the 'Experten', reaching this status either by sheer flying ability or a combination of being in the right place at the right time, flying ability and an aptitude for marksmanship. Once these men started to become established, the onus on their survival depended a great deal on the wingmen, who reaped little glory but provided most of the casualties.

As in most things there are exceptions to the rule, one of the most notable in this case being Oberfedwebel Steinbatz who flew as Oberst Graf's wingman. In June he received his Oak Leaves and his score stood at 99 when he was claimed by the notorious Russian anti-aircraft guns. It was this AA fire which caused most Luftwaffe pilots problems; although it is commented on in some depth by both dive and level bomber crews, the Jagdgruppen also quickly learned to respect the accuracy of the ground guns and without too much over generalisation, it is fair to claim that until the Red air force received better equipment and higher calibre pilots, the German fighter pilots lost a high percentage of their colleagues as a result of ground-to-air fire rather than air combat.

The closing weeks of 1942 saw the start of one of the most epic and well documented events of World War 2; the siege of Stalingrad. Although having successfully relieved Demyansk and Kholm from the air, Göring failed to appreciate the different circumstances which faced his transport Gruppen at Stalingrad, and it is well known that this relief operation failed so dismally that on February 2 1943 Generaloberst Paulus was forced to surrender and over 90,000 German troops fell into Russian hands. As far as the Jagdgruppen were concerned, this defeat was really the start of their decline. Units attempted to cover the aircraft taking supplies to the ground forces but gradually they were forced to withdraw from their airfields around Stalingrad, although for some six weeks a group of JG 3 pilots operated from Pitomnik claiming over 100 victories. But it was not so much the losses in action or the attrition which heralded the first seemingly insignificant appearance of the spectre of defeat, it was events in Germany. Instructors were transferred to the Russian front, thus curtailing the training programme, fuel became short and this resulted in a cut-back of all non-operational flying which also affected training. So, during 1944–45, although aircraft production reached its highest peak, there were fewer pilots to fly the new aircraft and insufficient fuel to operate them in any strength even if the crews had been available. These facts were not readily appreciated except by the very astute, who probably decided that it was unwise to voice them, so the Jagdgruppen continued to fight in much the same way as they had since 1941.

It is hard to suggest what alternatives faced them and any conclusions arrived at, such as a greater concentration in one particular part of the very long front line, or protection of German oil supply fields and routes, would probably not have altered the eventual outcome although it might have prolonged activity in certain areas.

The crushing defeat at Stalingrad and the set-backs in North Africa made Hitler determined to seek success in Russia and in an attempt to regain the initiative he mounted Operation 'Zitadelle'. This was aimed at Kursk and involved two simultaneous offensives in the northern and southern sectors. Luftflotte IV under General Otto Desslock provided 1,100 combat aircraft in the southern area and Fliegerdivision 1 under Generalmajor Paul Deichmann contributed 700 machines, the combined force representing just over 50 per cent of the available Luftwaffe strength in Russia at that time. The Soviets prepared their defences well and had over 2,400 aircraft ready to meet the Luftwaffe, among these being examples of the La 5 and Yak-9 fighters. What was to turn out to be the biggest conflict of armour in World War 2 started in the early morning of July 5 1943 when German tanks advanced on both fronts. Prior to this the Red air force had tried to catch Luftwaffe bombers on their airfields, but radar had warned of their intentions and fighters from JG 3, JG 54, JG 51 and JG 52 took a heavy toll of the raiders in what was the most intensive air activity since the opening days of 'Barbarossa'.

Although the ground battle went against the Germans, who by July 13 were forced to halt their advance and attempt to stabilise their line, the relatively small force of fighters continued to inflict considerable losses on the Red air force.

On July 13 Leutnant Erich Hartmann of 9/JG 52 claimed his 34th victory; not perhaps an important milestone for any pilot but in this case worth recording since he was destined to become a household name. Joining JG 52 in November 1942, Hartmann, flying one of the latest Bf 109Gs, achieved his first success on the 5th of the month, and by the time of his capture when the war ended in May 1945 he had claimed 352 victories, one of which, a Yak 11 on May 8, could well have been the last Luftwaffe aerial claim of the war. Every theatre of operations produced its aces and the legends which have developed around the exploits of Marseille in the Middle East have similarly surrounded Erich Hartmann, but in many ways to a higher degree since he is generally considered to be the highest scoring ace of all time.

His successes, coupled with those of his colleagues, did not influence the outcome of 'Zitadelle', and when during this operation USAAF bombers mounted the first of their famous daylight raids on the German homeland; and the RAF night raids mounted in intensity, the defence of the Reich began to take priority. Fighter units were withdrawn from all fronts to strengthen those already facing the USAAF/RAF onslaught, so as the Soviet air force increased in strength and improved equipment, it faced a sadly depleted adversary.

The quality of pilots and aircraft, which now included the latest G variants of the Bf 109 as well as the FW 190, did not, however, deteriorate, and the units left in the east fought tenaciously on all fronts. It is arguable whether they greatly influenced some of the battles of 1944–1945, because by this time it was obvious to all that the German cause was finished. But they certainly fought valiantly, not only in supporting the aircraft helping the army, but also in intercepting bombers which by 1943 were not only the Russian tactical types but also the USAAF and RAF

strategic forces engaged in either attacking oil refineries, overflying Russian territory, or attacking targets in Bulgaria, Hungary, Austria and southern Germany from Italian bases. They could not, of course, adequately cover such wide and diverse fronts and operational conditions, but together with the air forces of countries sympathetic to the German cause, which by now were being equipped with the best the German aircraft industry could produce, they did their very best and took a heavy toll.

It is very apparent to any student of this campaign that, at the end of the day, the salient feature of the German fighter pilots' war in Russian was very much individual success and this is supported by the large number of 'Experten' who emerged.

Men like Graf, Mölders, Rall, Munchberger, Nowotny, Hahn, Barkhorn, Lipfert, Hartmann and many others who achieved considerable individual success in this theatre, were supported by unsung heroes who contributed equally to their victories. All of them, whether or not they became 'Experten', faced the same problems which ranged from extreme cold to continuous rain; fine dust which got into everything including aero-engines and food; the fear of capture and worse still summary execution if they survived a crash and fell into the wrong hands; to perhaps the most demoralising factor of them all; continuous action. On the Russian front, fighter pilots were in the front line all the time; after a day's operations there was no question of a comfortable bed, a bath, a well prepared meal and maybe relaxation at the cinema or theatre: theirs was the same world of mud, snow, cold, damp and inadequate food of the infantryman.

The courage, tenacity, and individual success can only be admired and it must be remembered that these young men were only a cross-section of a country's youth who were involved in a war, whose origins they had no clear knowledge or particular views about. The majority of them became involved because of their love of flying, the skills they developed from this, and the inherent character which makes a fighter pilot, irrespective of the colour of his skin or uniform. The Luftwaffe Jagdgruppen achieved successes in Russia of which they can be proud; no fighting man or unit can ask for a more fitting epitaph.

ABOUT THE PHOTOGRAPHS

The photographs in this book have been selected with care from the Bundesarchiv, Koblenz (the approximate German equivalent of the US National Archives or the British Public Records Office). Particular attention has been devoted to choosing photographs which will be fresh to the majority of readers, although it is inevitable that one or two may be familiar. Other than this, the author's prime concern has been to choose good-quality photographs which illustrate the type of detail that enthusiasts and modellers require. In certain instances quality has, to a degree, been sacrificed in order to include a particularly interesting photograph. For the most part, however, the quality speaks for itself.

The Bundesarchiv files hold some one million black and white negatives of Wehrmacht and Luftwaffe subjects, including 150,000 on the Kriegsmarine, some 20,000 glass negatives from the inter-war period and several hundred colour photographs. Sheer numbers is one of the problems which makes the compilation of a book such as this difficult. Other difficulties include the fact that, in the vast majority of cases, the negatives have not been printed so the researcher is forced to look through box after box of 35 mm contact strips – some 250 boxes containing an average of over 5,000 pictures each, plus folders containing a further 115,000 contact prints of the Waffen-SS; moreover, cataloguing and indexing the negatives is neither an easy nor a short task, with the result that, at the present time, Luftwaffe and Wehrmacht subjects as well as entirely separate theatres of operations are intermingled in the same files.

There is a simple explanation for this confusion. The Bundesarchiv photographs were taken by war correspondents attached to German military units, and the negatives were originally stored in the Reich Propaganda Ministry in Berlin. Towards the close of World War 2, all the photographs – then numbering some $3\frac{1}{2}$ million – were ordered to be destroyed. One man in the Ministry, a Herr Evers, realised that they should be preserved for posterity and, acting entirely unofficially and on his own initiative, commandeered the first available suitable transport – two refrigerated fish trucks – loaded the negatives into them, and set out for safety. Unfortunately, one of the trucks disappeared en route and, to this day, nobody knows what happened to it. The remainder were captured by the Americans and shipped to Washington, where they remained for 20 years before the majority were returned to the government of West Germany. A large number, however, still reside in Washington. Thus the Bundesarchiv files are incomplete, with infuriating gaps for any researcher. Specifically, they end in the autumn of 1944, after Arnhem, and thus record none of the drama of the closing months of the war.

The photographs are currently housed in a modern office block in Koblenz, overlooking the River Mosel. The priceless negatives are stored in the basement, and there are strict security checks on anyone seeking admission to the Bildarchiv (Photo Archive). Regrettably, and the author has been asked to stress this point, the archives are *only open to bona fide authors and publishers, and prints can only be supplied for reproduction in a book or magazine.* They CANNOT be supplied to private collectors or enthusiasts for personal use, so *please* – don't write to the Bundesarchiv or the publishers of this book asking for copy prints, because they cannot be provided. The well-equipped photo laboratory at the Bundesarchiv is only capable of handling some 80 to 100 prints per day because each is printed individually under strictly controlled conditions – another reason for the fine quality of the photographs but also a contributory factor in the above legislation.

THE PHOTOGRAPHS

Left The Luftwaffe's top scoring ace, Major Erich Hartmann of JG 52. He ended the war as a prisoner of the Russians with 352 victories to his name, his last being a Yak 11 which he accounted for in the early morning on May 8 1945. His personal badge can be seen below the cockpit sill (503/353/17).

Above This FW 190A-4 of II/JG 54 has recently had a panel replaced to the left of the fuselage cross which is painted on a yellow tactical band. The aircraft in the background is a Finnish Air Force Brewster Buffalo (727/297/25).

Below The accessibility of the engine of the FW 190 is clearly visible in this shot of JG 54 mechanics working on an A-4 version. The cooling fan on the front of the engine can be clearly seen, and the two mechanics in the foreground are handling the oil cooler which fits inside the cowling's armoured ring (503/239/21).

Above Like all Luftwaffe fighters, the FW 190 was adapted for the fighter-bomber role. This machine in typical winter conditions is an A-5/U3 and carries a 500 kg bomb on its centre rack. The cowling ring is yellow as is the forward part of the spinner. The standard camouflage has been oversprayed white (500/102/7).

Below A very pleasing air-to-air shot taken over Rumania in early 1944 of an FW 190G-3 of II/SG 10 (500/106/16A).

Above This FW 190A-4 has lost most of its port wing in a wheels-up landing in February 1944. The aircraft is a I Gruppe machine and the black 7 indicates 3rd Staffel ownership (726/220/30).

Below Walter Nowotny, one of the Luftwaffe's leading 'Aces', in the cockpit of an FW 190A-6 of I/JG 54. The aircraft carries the Gruppe Kommandeur's chevrons before the fuselage cross which is painted on a yellow fuselage band; the stylised 73 in white below the cockpit is probably some form of personal marking (664/6789/26a).

Background photograph This impressive line-up of FW 190A-8s has previously been captioned as A-8/R2s, but there is no evidence of the underwing cupolas carrying MK 108 30 mm cannons which went with the R2 designation. The aircraft nearest the camera and the first one in the line carrying Gruppen Kommandeur markings have no Gruppen symbols behind their fuselage crosses, which would indicate I Gruppe aircraft (736/180/17a).

Inset above Hauptmann Moritz sits on the cockpit edge of his FW 190A-8. The additional armoured glass on the canopy sides is clearly visible, as is the retractable foot rest. This photograph was probably taken in the European theatre but is particularly good as far as camouflage and weathering of the aircraft is concerned. The wire hanging by the pilot's knee is in fact the radio lead to his helmet which dangles on the end (736/180/13A).

Inset right The 'kick' self-sealing foot rest, back parachute and canopy details provide useful information about both man and machine (500/125/35).

Above left This FW 190A-4 typifies most people's ideas of the Russian Front. The aircraft belongs to I/JG 54, the Gruppe badge being clearly visible on the cowling; the famous Grünherz badge of JG 54 is carried below the cockpit but cannot be seen in this photograph (623/3021/6a).

Left Part of the JG 54 badge referred to in the above photograph can be seen on one of the unit's FW 190A-4s. The pilot's fur-lined jacket and crew man's ear muffs underline the severity of the low temperature (624/3058/10a).

Above The very clean-looking FW 190A-4 displays typical Luftwaffe camouflage and fuselage markings which show it to be a III Gruppe aircraft. Once again this is probably a European theatre aircraft but both it and its pilot are representative of the high standards of equipment set by the Luftwaffe (625/3174/16a).

Right The badge of I/JG 54 adorns the cowling of this winter camouflaged FW 190A-4. The stripes are red and white, the background yellow and the eagle black. The winter clothing needs no comment (624/3058/33a).

Above They were a tough lot in the Luftwaffe! It was not all work and no play, and this impromptu revel in the snow seems to be causing a great deal of amusement among both the clothed and unclothed, although no doubt some of the latter probably regretted their actions later on (624/3061/14).

Below An FW 190A-4 of I/JG 54 on finals. The wing tips and fuselage bands are yellow as is the area under the cowling. The rudder appears to be a lighter shade of white than the rest of the aircraft but this is probably a trick of light caused by the application of some right rudder (625/3194/21).

Above Ground crew wait the pilot's signal to remove the wheel chocks from this A-4. The pilot will probably retract his flaps before taxiing as to leave them down invites damage from flying stones and other debris (625/3194/5).

Below Yellow painted inspection panels hang open beneath the cowling on this A-4 as a similar machine taxis by; note the flaps are retracted and the pilot's headgear matches the winter finish of his aircraft! (625/3156/10).

Left Hauptmann Horst Ademeit of I/JG 52 wearing winter overtrousers, a leather flight jacket under his life vest and the ever popular 'ski cap'. The aircraft is an A-4 and its Werke number is clearly visible on the rudder. Ademeit was killed on August 8 1944 when he was shot down in Russia by infantry fire (462/2137/31).

Below This FW 190 is an A-5 of I/JG 51 and is reputed to be the machine of Mölders, although whether or not he is the white helmeted figure in the cockpit is not known. The machine connected to the aircraft is heating essential equipment. Covers are still on the wings and tailplane (456/48/3a).

Right This A-4 has a very scruffy look about it, probably due to the whitewashed winter camouflage beginning to wear. The fuselage cross is on a band of the original camouflage and there are signs of a yellow band just forward of the tailplane. Wingtips and under surfaces of cowling are yellow (726/223/15a).

Below right What the well dressed FW 190G-8 wore to keep out the Russian winter. The very small wheel chocks are of interest (500/101/22a).

Left This picture reveals a wealth of detail each time it is studied. The pilot's back parachute, its rip-cord, the life jacket and the inflating bottle as well as tube, the Revi gunsight and part of the Infantry Support badge are just a few of the points worth noting (332/3096/39).

Below A salvage crew tries to recover usable parts from an FW 190, probably on the European front. Nonetheless, the overall structure of the aircraft was the same in every theatre. The black triangle ahead of the fuselage cross indicates a Schlact Gruppen aircraft, its position ahead of the cross shows it to be a I Gruppe machine (333/3104/3a).

Right Servicing time for an A-4. Engine accessibility, both through the large cowlings and from the ground where the lower parts were within easy reach of a standing man, made the FW 190 very popular with Luftwaffe ground crew (664/6789/11a).

Above A Feldwebel is helped with his parachute harness before embarking on a ground attack mission. The aircraft is an A-5 with an SC 500 bomb on its ETC 500 centre-line rack (503/238/25a).

Below Two FW 190s of II Gruppe of an unknown unit await the take-off signal from the fur-coated controller holding the flag. The aircraft in the foreground carries its bomb load on a centre-line rack, whilst the one behind has bombs on wing racks. The propeller to the right belongs to a Bf 109 (500/107/23a).

Above right The 'Tatzel Wurm' seen on the cowling of this FW 190 was used by I/JG 3 and later by II/JG 1, to which this aircraft belongs. It was customary to paint the symbol in the Staffel colour which in this case was yellow. The aircraft has ETC 71 wing racks outboard of the undercarriage. The covers have been removed from the wheels to prevent snow getting between the spats and wheels (503/213/12a).

Right Two mechanics struggle with an ammunition box to complete the re-arming of this A-5. The SC 50 bomb has whistles attached to its fins. Removal of the wheel spat shows useful detail of the shock absorber, caliper and brake pipe (332/3094/29).

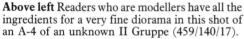

Above left Readers who are modellers have all the ingredients for a very fine diorama in this shot of an A-4 of an unknown II Gruppe (459/140/17).

Left The characteristic armoured cowling ring, stalky undercarriage and engine accessibility are all very clear on these II Gruppe A-4s (459/140/22).

Above Battle damage to the tail of this A-4 comes under close scrutiny from (probably) the pilot (the Leutnant leaning on the tailplane), an Unteroffizier wearing the peaked cap and two Fliegers who will probably end up carrying out the repair work (464/381/30a).

Above right The tropical filter indicates that this is not an Eastern front aircraft, but the 20 mm ammunition and cowling details make it a worthwhile inclusion (332/3096/28).

Right The pilot of this I Gruppe ground attack FW 190 watches intently as a mechanic makes some form of adjustment to the inboard gun inspection panel and another moves forward with a centre-line bomb (333/3104/4a).

Above An old barn provides some shelter from the elements for this FW 190 whose tail is protected by what has been recorded as a parachute but is in fact some form of canvas (459/140/23).

Below The oversprayed white winter finish is practically worn away on this A-5 whose empty fuselage rack indicates the end of a ground attack sortie. The A-5 was some five inches longer than the A-4 and could be identified by an additional wing fillet forward of the wing root, which can be seen in this photograph with the aid of a magnifying glass (623/3039/30a).

Above A fine assortment of flying gear is to be seen as the four pilots on the right listen to the Luftwaffe version of 'and there I was upside down . . .' (727/285/22a).

Below The II Gruppe Operations Officer has the guns of his FW 190A-4 tested in the firing butts (727/280/24A).

Above A Bf 109E-4 of II/JG 54 on the Leningrad front in 1941 throws up some interesting anomalies. It is a II Gruppe aircraft but does not carry the Gruppe symbol behind the fuselage cross, the chevron is the Gruppe Adjutant's and in addition to the vertical bar it carries the code 5. The badge below the cockpit is the personal emblem of Leutnant Steindl and that below the windscreen is the Lion of Aspern. The officers watching the operation are Hauptmann Harbok and Oberleutnant Philippe (534/26/20a).

Below left The I Gruppe badge on the nose of this Bf 109E has been almost obliterated by the winter camouflage. The heart below the cockpit is the famous 'Grünherz' of JG 54 (623/3021/3a).

This page When the snow thawed the result was lots and lots of glorious mud—although it is doubtful if Luftwaffe crews viewed it in this light! The aircraft being pushed into its muddy dispersal is a Bf 109G-6 of JG 3 (634/3890/3 and 7).

Above This late G model Bf 109 is having winter camouflage sprayed over its customary splinter and mottle. The stencil used for its individual Staffel number is on the tailplane, and it looks as though the canopy has been completely removed. The 'package' on the wing is a parachute, and the ring on the top fuselage is a loop aerial used for direction finding; the mast for the communications aerial would be forward of this and has probably been temporarily removed (666/6893/19a).

Below This is a very early war posed photograph of refuelling a Bf 109D and was used in handling manuals (335/25/24).

Above The service area on a forward Luftwaffe base. Aircraft with its cowlings removed is a Bf 109F (506/82/24).

Below Another kill marking is added to the rudder of a I(J)/LG 2 Bf 109E in Rumania. The soft spray line between camouflage colours shows that a hard mask line was not used in every case (MSO 2/86/6).

Above The detail of cockpit framing, rivet lines and wear and tear on the camouflage, will no doubt be welcomed by the fastidious modeller. Aircraft is a Bf 109G (499/57/1a).

Below Gerhard Barkhorn, who ended the war with 301 victories, is seen here in the uniform of a Leutnant. His pilot's badge is below the Iron Cross First Class on his left breast and the badge above is a mission clasp (502/176/25).

Above Barkhorn in his Bf 109G-5. This photograph is worth comparing with the one in *Photo Album No 4*, page 25, which shows that although they appear to be the same machine they are probably not as the position of the name 'Christl' below the cockpit differs (502/776/18).
Below Leutnant Barkhorn and another JG 52 pilot stand before the former's Bf 109 and celebrate his 1,000th operational flight (502/177/15A).

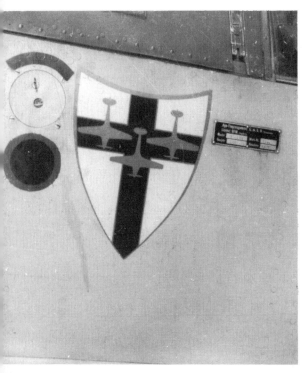

Above A Bf 109F 'Red 1' of the Staffelkapitän of 8/JG 54. The pilot striding away from the aircraft is wearing a one-piece flying suit which is more usually associated with bomber crews. The man on the wing is a Stabsfeldwebel (Warrant Officer). The badge forward of the cockpit is the Staffel badge and the one on the engine cowling a personal emblem (395/1533/28a).

Left This badge carried by a III/JG 27 Bf 109, Werke No 3344, is identical to that carried by aircraft of II/JG 54 in Russia, only the colours differed. In this case the badge, which is on a Middle East Theatre aircraft, is yellow with a black cross on which are superimposed three yellow 109s. The JG 54 badge mentioned is clearly visible in the previous picture (335/21/15).

Above right Armourers load the fuselage-mounted MG 131 machine-guns of Erich Hartmann's Bf 109G (see also page 14) (505/373/13a).

Right It is said that man's best friend is a dog; Erich Hartmann seems to share this view. The rank epaulettes show that he was an Oberleutnant when this particular photograph was taken (505/358/12A).

Far right A hot meal for the 'blond knight of Germany' (505/373/15a).

Above left The Bf 109G flown by Erich Hartmann when he was an Oberleutnant. His personal emblem, a heart with an arrow through it, can be seen just below the cockpit windscreen (503/232/10a).

Left Leutnant Erwin Leykauf looks somewhat pensive as he poses by the Bf 109F of the III Gruppe Kommandeur. The badge above the exhaust stack is the arms of the City of Ansbach (396/1623/10a).

Above The pilot of this Royal Rumanian Air Force Bf 109G poses for the cameraman before setting off on a sortie. The Luftwaffe crewman near the wing root carries the rank insignia of a Gefreiter (635/3958/6).

Right Uniform detail and the Mickey Mouse insignia as well as the cockpit and inboard flap of this Bf 109G-5 provide useful modelling details. The pilot is Hauptmann Horst Carganico of II/JG 5 which was operating in the Arctic when this photograph was taken (506/82/7).

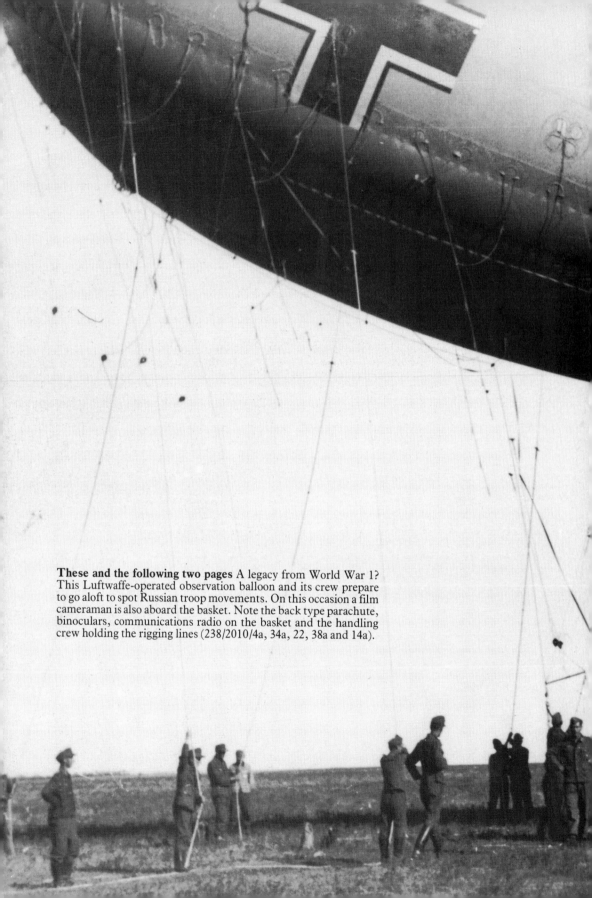

These and the following two pages A legacy from World War 1? This Luftwaffe-operated observation balloon and its crew prepare to go aloft to spot Russian troop movements. On this occasion a film cameraman is also aboard the basket. Note the back type parachute, binoculars, communications radio on the basket and the handling crew holding the rigging lines (238/2010/4a, 34a, 22, 38a and 14a).

Above left A Bf 109E-3 of I(J)LG 2 photographed in Rumania in 1941 (MSO/86/5).

Left Although the quality of this photograph is somewhat lacking when compared with others, it does show a rather unusual camouflage scheme; it is also interesting to note that the aircraft has had its wheel covers removed, a common practice in snowy wintery conditions (459/132/32).

Above The III Gruppe symbol is evident behind the fuselage cross in this very good shot of a G-6 setting out on a sortie. The lumps and bumps apparent on the airframe contrast with the smooth lines of the earlier E and F models. The G was the most produced version of the Bf 109 (659/6411/5a).

Right The intense cold of the Russian winter made proper clothing essential. This Leutnant has the ideal overcoat which is being worn over his tunic and flying suit. The boots are standard issue flying wear (503/213/16a).

Background photograph A Bf 109G-6 of an unknown unit being serviced in a rather bleak and forbidding environment (503/232/9a).

Inset The mottle camouflage and simplified fuselage cross is shown to advantage on this Bf 109G-2 (499/57/6A).

Above The narrow track undercarriage, centre-line drop tank and aileron mass balance are all very clear in this attractive view of the G-6 of the II Gruppe Kommandeur of JG 54 (460/194/25).

Below A Bf 109G has its fuselage-mounted guns tested in the firing butts. The gantry supporting the aircraft and the rod passing through the rear fuselage are of interest. The noise must have been colossal but it does not seem to be worrying the two observers, one of whom appears to be filming the scene (680/825/27).

Above Winter camouflage was a coat of water soluble paint sprayed over the normal finish; naturally this wore very quickly and soon became very patchy. Aircraft is a G-6 (667/7110/29a).

Below The rather broad-shouldered Hauptmann sitting in the cockpit of this G-6 illustrates the cramped 'office' which is often commented on by Luftwaffe pilots. The open leading edge slots are clearly visible as is the simplified white outline cross on the top wing surface (727/282/11a).

Above I Gruppe aircraft of an unknown Bf 109-equipped Jagdgeschwader are prepared for the day's work on a typical bleak airfield. The fuselage band on which the cross is painted is yellow (725/177/27a).

Below A lot of controversy has surrounded the designation of certain late mark Bf 109s, some late Gs with tall fins and rudders being called Ks and vice versa. It is believed that this aircraft, which clearly has the taller fin/rudder and so called 'Galland' hood, is a Bf 109G-14 (505/353/3a).

Above The Luftwaffe used several styles of lettering for aircraft numbering. This Bf 109G, believed to be called 'TOSCA', illustrates one style of '4' used regularly (506/82/20).

Below A half-track is used to recover a Bf 109G which has recently carried out an emergency landing as evidenced by the bent propeller blades. The wheel spats have been removed revealing a somewhat stalky looking pair of oleos (634/3873/33).

Größt zulässiger Reifen 65

Left A Hauptmann, whose aircraft carries the Gruppen Kommandeur's chevrons, dons his flight blouse on which can be clearly seen his rank badge (454/1066/18).

Above A G-6 stirs up the snow as it moves out under the watchful gaze of the mechanic on the wing tip. The under surfaces of the tips are painted yellow (456/48/12).

Below A temporarily discarded cutting machine helps to add an air of unreality to this winter scene which captures the conditions faced by men and machines. The aircraft is a Bf 109G with a yellow painted fuselage band and white 8 (456/48/10).

Above left Leutnant Woidisch of I/JG 52 prepares to climb aboard his Bf 109G whilst the man on the right stands by the starting handle (498/39/27a).

Left Possibly a Bf 109G-10/U4, this aircraft is of interest since what appears to be a standard 66 Imperial gallon drop tank has a clear perspex nose cone. Could it be that this was some form of reconnaissance pack? (680/8264/15).

Above A busy winter activity scene which illustrates very well the removed wheel covers and associated oleo details (630/3584/11).

Right The removeable fuselage hatch gave easy access to the Bf 109's radio equipment and other close-by components as well as control runs. The interior probably gave some much welcome respite to the mechanic who perhaps didn't realise just how much the end was in sight! (459/140/32).

Left The white outline to the aircraft's code number is added with some precision by two very young airmen (499/57/3).

Below This Bf 109G appears to be carrying out a wheels-up landing, but the spray thrown up from the snow simply hides the aircraft's main gear (503/228/15a).

Right Two 109Gs stand idle as He 111s pressed into the transport role join the landing pattern at this forward airfield (500/107/22a).

Below right Accessibility to the DB 605 engine of the 109G was achieved through removeable cowlings both top and bottom. In this view the lower cowling has been opened and the port top cowling lifted (459/136/30a).

Left The top surface splinter camouflage and yellow fuselage band are very prominent in this air-to-air of a Bf 109G-6 high above the Russian countryside (727/283/37a).

Below left Yellow 12 of the third Staffel of I/JG 54 waits for the wheel chocks to be removed as an FW 190 wheels overhead (624/3058/8a).

Right The ever-popular spiral spinner decoration appears this time on a Bf 109G whose Feldwebel (Sergeant) pilot displays a somewhat fancy line in headgear. Once again the wheel spats have been removed (459/732/27).

Below Snow always seems to add a certain charm to any type of picture, no doubt it was cursed as much by these mechanics as it is by those of us today who are occasionally inconvenienced by it. The removed panels, wooden runners and general paraphernalia surrounding this Bf 109G all add interest to the scene (459/140/30).

Above The starboard wheel of this Bf 109G has just been changed and perhaps the three men sitting on the port wing are waiting the arrival of some equipment to enable them to carry out work on the engine, whose intricate plumbing is clearly visible (635/3951/39).

Left Rudimentary air traffic control as carried out by two well wrapped-up airmen. The flag indicates the wind direction and the white board carrying the letter L was used for visual communication with pilots. In this case it looks as though radio communication has been established (625/3194/12).

Above right The Luftwaffe equivalent to the perforated steel runways used by the Allies is used to form a steady surface on which this Bf 109G-6 can be moved. One interesting aspect is that, on the leading edges of most 109s, there were stencil instructions to the effect 'Do Not Push Here' (727/282/13).

Right A III Gruppe Bf 109G-2 which appears to have had a former unit's badge painted out (641/4531/26).

Above and above right Finnish fighter squadrons equipped with the American-built Brewster Buffalo also fought against the Russians. These two views show very clearly the national markings, camouflage and many other small details (727/297/25a and 28).

Left The significance of the model is not known but it seems to be a well made metal one so could be an award to the pilot by his squadron colleagues. Close-up detail of his life vest is worthy of note (625/3174/39a).

Right Major Erich Rudorffer, the Kommandeur of II/JG 54. He survived the war with 222 victories and was shot down on 16 occasions. Rudorffer became the Kommandeur of II/JG 7 flying Me 262 jet fighters (727/297/36).

Cumulonimbus

This page and above right Cartoons feature very prominently in most air forces' official and unofficial publications. Pilot Officer Prune was an RAF wartime favourite who appeared in *Tee Em*, his antics being a lesson to the unwary. The Luftwaffe too had their equivalent and extracts from the magazine were often to be seen adorning crew rooms. These examples photographed in JG 54's crew room on a Russian airfield graphically illustrate types of cloud and the dangers of dreaming when on ops (533/10/1a, 20 and 21).

Right Two of the Luftwaffe's most famous aces discuss points: Major Walter Nowotny, at this time an Oberleutnant, on the wing, and Oberst Hannes Trautloft, the Kommodore of JG 54, in the cockpit (460/194/17).

Far right Walter Nowotny in the uniform of an Oberleutnant. His rank is shown by the collar tabs and epaulettes. The badge above his left pocket is a mission clasp and at his neck he wears the Knight's Cross (460/194/20).

Alto - Cumulus

Background photograph The RAF gave the Russian air force some Hurricanes in an attempt to put them on more even terms with the Luftwaffe's superior fighters. The Russians did, on some occasions, put these to good use but the Hurricane was no real match for the later mark Bf 109s. These two are derelict reminders of the Allied aid to the Red air force (216/446/6a).

Inset right Hauptmann Heinz Frank, an FW 190 pilot of SG 2, showing the Luftwaffe officer's service cap and leather flight jacket. He wears the Knight's Cross with oakleaves (500/104/7a).

Inset far right An alternative flight jacket worn by Leutnant Gunther Müller, an Hs 129 pilot whose decoration is a Knight's Cross (500/107/9a).

Above left A wounded fighter pilot is returned to his unit by a Luftwaffe reconnaissance patrol mounted on a Zundapp combination (682/34/21a).

Left A Flak 88 is trundled past a Bf 109G which has the diamond outline of the badge carried by JG 51 and JG 5; in the case of the former the centre is the Ace of Spades, while the latter is a four-leafed clover (458/88/10).

This page Two vastly contrasting forms of transport used by the Luftwaffe to travel the frozen wastes. The three man-power wooden sled carries ammunition boxes whilst the snowmobile is being used for casualty evacuation (459/136/22a and 622/2976/13a).

Left JG 54 improvised a sauna for use by crews who were hardy enough to dash from the heated cabin into the snow. The entrance is decorated by the Geschwader badge, and other artwork flanks the temperature gauge (624/3061/26).

Below A 250-round ammunition box removed from a Hurricane. This was photographed by the Luftwaffe at Okezie on September 17 1944 (LOC 436).

Right Oberleutnant Friedrich Obliser of JG 52. The fighter pilot's mission clasp and his Knight's Cross are clearly visible (505/353/22).

Far right Hauptmann Heinz Frank prepares for another ground attack sortie in his FW 190 of SG 2. The safety harness can be seen hanging over the cockpit edge, and the fully castoring tailwheel is currently across the line of flight (500/104/30a).

Below right Erich Hartmann's Bf 109G-6 being loaded by armourers whose 'dress' shows that it was not always cold on the Eastern Front (505/373/11a).

Left and above The Rumanian air force operated alongside the Luftwaffe in their IAR 80Cs in which the Oerlikon cannons were replaced by MG 151s. The attractive lines of the aircraft are very evident in these two views of No 243 being prepared for a sortie. The clear canopy, reflector sight, position of the radio aerial and the tail skid are all noteworthy points (498/25/20a and 19a).

Right Battle damage to a Bf 109G is repaired by an airframe fitter well protected for such work in what must have been very trying conditions. The circular panel to the left of the 5 is for filling the aircraft's oxygen cylinders (459/140/30a).

Above An Il 2 Stormovik ground attack aircraft wings its way towards German armour but in so doing fails to safely negotiate the gauntlet of German fighter cover and falls a victim to an FW 190 (213/290/13a).

Below The Il 2 illustrated above being examined by Luftwaffe personnel who are removing its ammunition (505/387/11a).

Opposite page The Il 2 was a sturdy aircraft and could take a lot of punishment; the tail unit of this machine broke away during its crash landing (635/3957/35 and 34).

Above left Hermann Göring has obviously said something to amuse the Oberfeldwebel pilot who wears a Knight's Cross and an Iron Cross 1st Class. Alongside his pilot's badge he wears the glider pilot's 'C' certificate qualification badge (659/6428/24).

Left and this page This series of photographs show that the Bf 110 could take a lot of damage and return to fight another day. This aircraft belongs to the 4th Staffel of II/ZG 76 and was not photographed on the Eastern front; nonetheless it does illustrate the sturdy structure of the machine which did not suffer nearly so badly in Russia as it did at the hands of RAF fighters during August 1940 (663/6740/36, 37 and 38).

Above The armoured windscreen of this Bf 110G-2, and the pilot's roll bar are two items often overlooked when studying general shots of the aircraft (662/6658/12a).

Below The crew of this Bf 110G-2/R6 relax under the wing of their machine which carries a twin MG 151 ventral pack and twin Wfr Gr 21 rocket launching tubes under each mainplane (649/5369/41).

Right The business end of a Bf 110F-1 (643/4753/6a).

Left A Bf 109 approaches over two F models of its twin-engined cousin. The 110's most notable successes came in the night fighting role, but it did perform very well on the Eastern front in both the long range fighter and ground attack roles (212/228/6a).

Below left Another very clear view of the armoured windscreen and roll bar first introduced on the Bf 110F. The pilot is having his straps adjusted by a mechanic and ahead of him can be seen the Revi reflector sight (643/4753/4a).

Right Access to the rear cockpit of the Bf 110 was tricky, especially when wearing full flying kit including a bulky parachute harness (211/172/6a).

Below The rear gunner of a Bf 110 adjusts his 7.9 mm rear defensive machine-gun which is on an Arado flexible mounting. Trying to aim and fire this gun in a twisting, diving aircraft must have been extremely difficult (643/4753/16a).

Left The radio compartment of a Bf 110 showing the very basic seat for the crew member and the rear of the pilot's armoured seat (643/4753/13a).

Above The revised crew entry to the rear compartment on the G model of the Bf 110 is very evident in this picture of a G-2. Rear armament is now a pair of 7.9 mm MG 81Z machine-guns (238/2011/9).

Below A garland and suitably inscribed legend reflect the joy of this Bf 110G pilot who has just completed his unit's 2,000th operational flight. The gun barrels appear to be dummies which was often the case in aircraft carrying out the reconnaissance role (459/144/35).

These pages The cameraman was present to record the incident shown in these photographs when this Bf 110G-2 fighter bomber conveniently burst into flames when its port DB605 engine was started. The series of photographs show the pilot hurriedly evacuating the cockpit, the ground crew moving cautiously with the fire fighting equipment, and the complete dousing of the fire helped by one of the aircrew, who can be seen still wearing his flying equipment directing an extinguisher into the engine. The aircraft is coded Q1 + VB and the skeletal markings extend over the top surfaces of the engine cowlings as well as the nose (238/2011/21, 14, 15 and 17).

Opposite page The pilot of this G-2, which is from the same unit as that shown on the previous page, celebrates either the completion of his time in Southern Russia, or more likely a landmark in the unit's achievements. Any reader with accurate information concerning the situation and markings of the aircraft is invited to get in touch with the author via the publishers (283/2011/29 and 26).

Right The observer of the G-2 mentioned in the above caption leaves the aircraft on which it is possible to see the extent of the skeletal markings on the top surfaces of the cowlings. The weapon in the rear cockpit is a twin 7.9 mm MG 81Z (238/2011/12).

Above The method of hinging for the gunner's hood on the C, D and F models of the Bf 110 can be appreciated from this view of an Unteroffizier gunner collecting equipment from a ground crew airman. The aircraft's first aid stowage compartment is clearly marked (211/172/10).

Above Infantry support aircraft like this Hs 123 could operate safely only when the Jagdgeschwader controlled the sky. In Russia, especially in the early days of the campaign, the Luftwaffe fighters had total control, thus enabling pilots of these somewhat antique-looking biplanes to go about their task with impunity. The badge is the Infanterie-Sturmabzeichen emblem which was carried by many ground attack aircraft (333/3104/24a).

Below Another very successful aircraft used to support the ground forces was the Hs 129. This aircraft is a B-2/R2 version of SG 9 and the pilot is Hauptmann Rudolf Ruffer. The gunsight is located on the nose in front of the windscreen and the aircraft is very heavily armoured as is evident by the pilot's seat (505/352/23a).

Above The upturned engine exhausts and ungainly lines of the engine cowlings of this C-4 are worth comparing with the smoother cowls of the later F and even more improved lines of the G, photographs of which can be found in this and other books in the series. The pilot of the aircraft is the centre kneeling figure and carries the rank insignia of a Hauptmann, the man to his right being a Feldwebel (534/18/10).

Below The rather pleasing lines of the Bf 109G are well illustrated in this view of an aircraft on final approach. The picture also accentuates the machine's very narrow track undercarriage (625/3194/22).

1. Representative Luftwaffe fighter data

Messerschmitt Bf 109G–6
Span: 32 feet 6½ inches. Length: 29 feet 8 inches.
Engine: One Daimler-Benz DB605A–1 12-cylinder, liquid-cooled, inverted V.
Performance: 387 mph at 22,000 feet. Maximum ceiling: 39,750 feet.
Armament: Two 13 mm|MG 131 with 300 rpg, one 20 mm MG 151 with 150 rounds, and two 20 mm MG 151 with 120 rpg in underwing gondolas.

Focke-Wulf FW 190A–4
Span: 34 feet 5½inches. Length: 29 feet 4 inches.
Engine: One BMW 801D–2 14-cylinder, air-cooled radial.
Performance: 400 mph at 20,000 feet. Maximum ceiling: 38,400 feet.
Armament: Two 7.9 mm MG 17 with 1,000 rpg, two 20 mm MG 151 with 200 rpg, two 20 mm MG FF with 55 rpg.

2. Fighter units and their equipment at the opening of Operation 'Barbarossa', June 22 1941

Luftflotte 1
JG 54   Stab, I, II and III Gruppen—Bf 109E/F
JG 53   II Gruppe—Bf 109F

Luftflotte 2
JG 51   Stab, I, II and III Gruppen—Bf 109F
SKG 210   I, II Gruppen—Bf 110
JG 27   II and III Gruppen—Bf 109E
JG 53   III Gruppe—Bf 110
JG 52   II Gruppe—Bf 110
ZG 26   I and II Gruppen—Bf 110

Luftflotte 4
JG 52   Stab, I and II—Bf 109F
JG 3   Stab, I, II, III—Bf 109F
LG 2   I(Jagd) Gruppe—Bf 109F
JG 77   Stab, II and III Gruppen—Bf 109E

Luftflotte 5
JG 77   I Gruppe and one Staffel of IV Gruppe—Bf 109E
JG 1   III Gruppe—Bf 109E
ZG 76   I Gruppe—Bf 110

3. Highest scoring aces

The listed pilots scored over 200 victories including the following achieved on the Russian front; the difference between those shown here and those listed in World War 2 *Photo Album No 4*, Appendix 3, are victories in other theatres.

Major Erich Hartmann	352
Major Gerhard Barkhorn	301
Major Günther Rall	271
Oberleutnant Otto Kittel	267
Major Walter Nowotny	255
Major Wilhelm Batz	237
Oberst Heinrich Ehrler	204
Hauptmann Helmut Lipfert	203
Oberst Hermann Graf	202
Oberleutnant Walter Schuck	198

ACHTUNG! COMPLETED YOUR COLLECTION?

Other titles in the same series

No 1 Panzers in the Desert
by Bruce Quarrie

No 2 German Bombers over England
by Bryan Philpott

No 3 Waffen-SS in Russia
by Bruce Quarrie

No 4 Fighters Defending the Reich
by Bryan Philpott

No 5 Panzers in North-West Europe
by Bruce Quarrie

No 6 German Fighters over the Med
by Bryan Philpott

No 7 German Paratroops in the Med
by Bruce Quarrie

No 8 German Bombers over Russia
by Bryan Philpott

No 9 Panzers in Russia 1941–43
by Bruce Quarrie

No 10 German Fighters over England
by Bryan Philpott

No 11 U-Boats in the Atlantic
by Paul Beaver

No 12 Panzers in Russia 1943–45
by Bruce Quarrie

No 13 German Bombers over the Med
by Bryan Philpott

No 14 German Capital Ships
by Paul Beaver

No 15 German Mountain Troops
by Bruce Quarrie

In preparation

No 17 E-Boats and Coastal Craft
by Paul Beaver

No 18 German Maritime Aircraft
by Bryan Philpott

No 19 Panzers in the Balkans and Italy
by Bruce Quarrie

No 20 German Destroyers and Escorts
by Paul Beaver

ACHTUNG! COMPLETED YOUR COLLECTION?